Maz Hakim is the daughter of Afghan parents who risked everything by fleeing the war and immigrating to Australia. Maz discovered her love of sharing stories through her nearly decade-long radio career. She expresses herself through various artforms, including the creation of her one-of-a-kind clothing range, jewelry design, and poetry. She is a long-time radio presenter on Dubai's number 1 radio station.

Maz Hakim

GREEN SPACE

Austin Macauley Publishers™
LONDON • CAMBRIDGE • NEW YORK • SHARJAH

Copyright © Maz Hakim 2022
Illustrated by Lena Kassicieh

The right of **Maz Hakim** and **Lena Kassicieh** to be identified as author and illustrator of this work has been asserted by them in accordance with Federal Law No. (7) of UAE, Year 2002, Concerning Copyrights and Neighboring Rights.

All rights reserved. No part of this publication may be reproduced, stored in a retrieval system, or transmitted in any form or by any means, electronic, mechanical, photocopying, recording, or otherwise, without the prior permission of the publishers.

Any person who commits any unauthorized act in relation to this publication may be liable to legal prosecution and civil claims for damages.

The age group that matches the content of the books has been classified according to the age classification system issued by the National Media Council.

ISBN - 9789948825869 - (Paperback)
ISBN - 9789948825876 - (E-book)

Application Number: MC-10-01-2564769
Age Classification: E

Printer Name: iPrint Global Ltd
Printer Address: Witchford, England

First Published 2022
AUSTIN MACAULEY PUBLISHERS FZE
Sharjah Publishing City
PO Box [519201]
Sharjah, UAE
www.austinmacauley.ae
+971 655 95 202

Safe Skies

For not accepting war in your children's future

For bravely fleeing across mountains to start anew

For your tireless efforts to fight your way to freedom

For sacrificing your own goals to build us a safe nest

For watching on as we spread our wings

Mom and Dad, this is for you.

There is no instruction book to succeed in life

It stubbornly requires much trial and error

We make mistakes... but that increases knowledge

We get hurt... but that increases wisdom

Crops fail... but fertile land abounds

And sunshine is plentiful!

King or common man
Kufr or din

Without love
Life is a sin.

Loveless Sin

Thank you for showing me I'm
capable to feel
That my delicate heart I would allow someone to steal.

Thank you for the rollercoaster ride
But we weren't capable of surviving the tide.

Thank you for making me strong
But I no longer hear you in every song.

Bittersweet moments that taught me to grow
And the aftermath has allowed me to glow.

Homage to a chapter that is now dead
No more thorns, just a floral path ahead.

Homage

Your dreams and my dreams
And your dreams and mine

Two visions we couldn't combine.

But a beautiful thing emerged out of the two
Two separate fruitful paths

One for me and one for you.

Fruitful

Your name was written on the walls of my heart
Now it's just graffiti
And no longer art.

Graffiti

It's a Full moon tonight
Shining high and shining bright

I look up at the sky
And wonder why

It's the only thing we still share.

Between Us

We are on and off
'round and 'round
Our relationship is like a nauseous merry go round.

In Circles

Tonight when you aren't near me
It's like my third eye can't see.

Third Eye

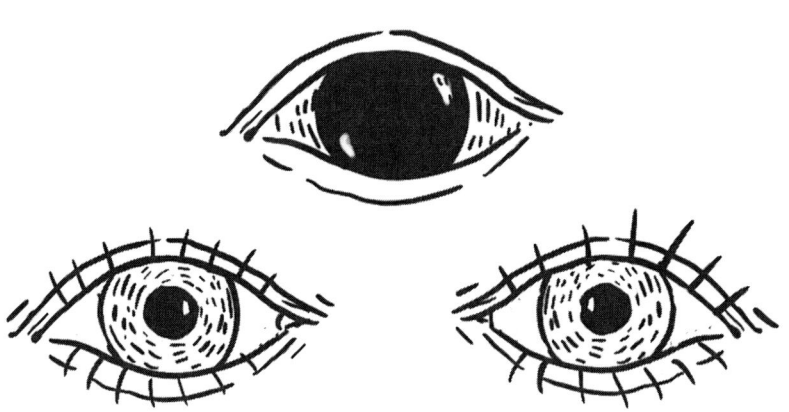

Twin flame
Set you alight

Burn you bright
An internal fight

Love, lust, passion and pain
So much loss
And not enough gain

An invisible chord
Between the two

Teachings and lessons
Learning about you

Growth and joy
Sweet and sour

The kind of love
That takes your power.

Twin Flame

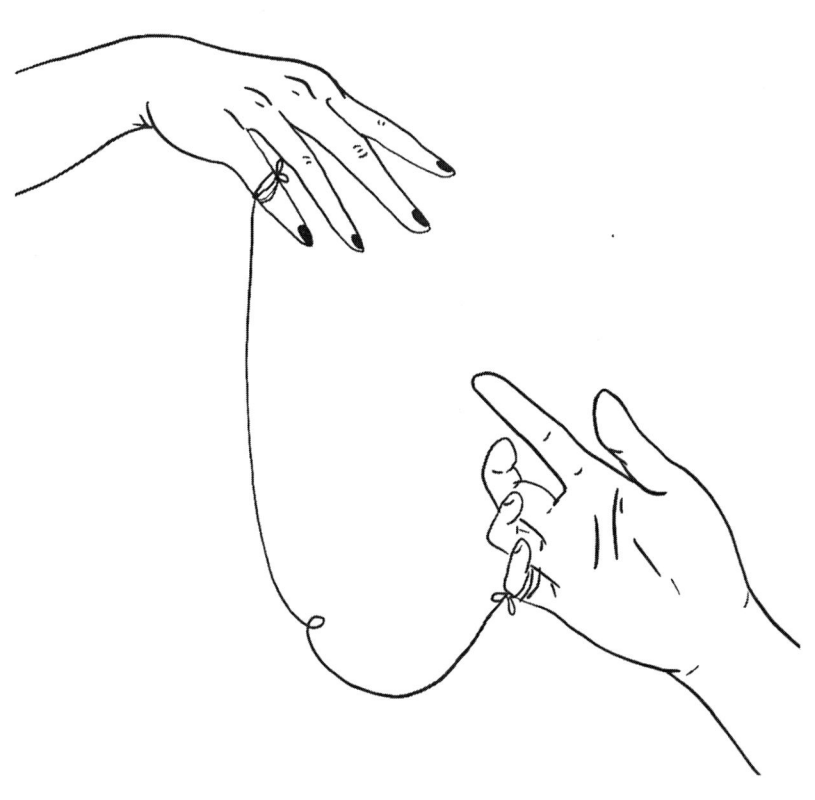

For the next woman you meet I'll give you some words

Speak with love, speak with kind
because all these words remain in her mind.

There's a saying by Rumi, an ancient Persian poet
And I've said this to you before and that's why you should know it.

"Raise your words, not voice. It is rain that grows flowers, not thunder."

Thunder

Screaming is a form of self defense
But there are other ways to deal with things if you're tense.

Losing grasp of your voice is like losing control
And hurting someone else and their soul.

When you scream at flowers, they won't grow, plants they whittle and flowers die
But humans in response…they'll just cry.

Things can be replaced, money can be earnt
But when love is real, the screaming must be unlearnt.

Screaming

In a room full of people
And I can still feel you.

Flashing lights, the treble, and bass
Sewing palm trees, sand, and the glistening sunset.

Picture perfect, but is it really?

Crowds of people but I still feel your presence
No, you can't keep lovers apart.

Walking through the crowds, faces that don't feel like home
Nobody here that feels like my own.

Crowds

Cruel and cold
Gentle and kind

Show me both sides of your mind.

Cruel Intentions

Can't wait to wake up and have black coffee with you
Standing in the kitchen, just us two.

Talking about life and our plans together
The future so bright, as light as a feather.

As I lie here listening to music in the back of the car
Thinking about you, because you are now so far.

I'm romantic and I can't help it
Bollywood and Disney, but I don't regret it.

Capri, Luxembourg, Dubai, London, who knows what the future holds
But making plans is for the bold.

Whatever happens I hope we are in this for the long run
Maria and Riccardo shining bright like the sun.

There's something in Farsi we called kis-mat
Which means if it's meant to be, it will happen without a but.

Ricardo

My love, I'm going to set you completely free
Because together we were obviously never meant to be.

You can go and do as you please
And give someone else your heart and your keys.

Set You Free

When I close my eyes, I can feel you next to me
Your presence gives me a sense of Chi.

You're a rock that makes me feel balanced
Every home with you is a palace.

Chi

Euros in millions and high GDPs
Crisp suits with no soul
Success without the one you love
Is a failed goal.

Corporate

Beats 100,000 times a day
Each pump for who.

Under the chest that has your name
Layers of armor that couldn't protect.

Skin and bones that let me down
A queen that now put down her crown.

Take the tightness away
That comes and goes

Of a heart in pain
The pain that does not show.

Heartache

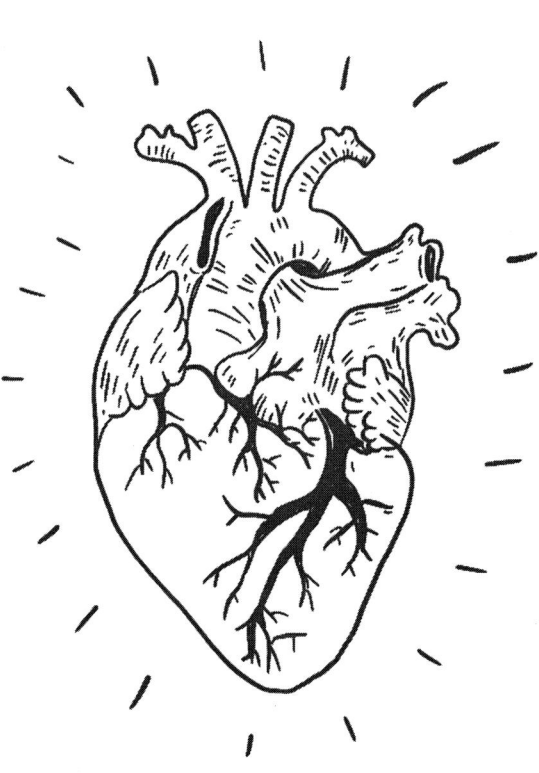

You said you would
But you didn't call.

You said you would catch me
If I ever fall.

Falling

You said we would be together
I the bird, you my feather.

You said we would fly side by side
And that one day I would be your bride.

Feathers

I tried consoling my heart
With songs
And poems
And food.

But how do you heal a heart
When it's been taken away from you?

Stolen

Your voluminous hair shines tall and bright
I heard about your lovers throughout the night.

Don't forget me, apple
The old want in my eye.

Though I still love you
I will never reply.

Old Love

We tend to push people away when we need them the most
We should want support at the time of trauma and not post.

Like when a turtle hides away in its shell
We bury our emotions and pretend we are fine and well.

When people love you, they want to be there
Not pushed away, and from afar they stare.

From Afar

Stay out of my dreams
Stop stealing my sleep

Just let me escape
To a place I can't weep.

Sleep

The female soul is such an enchanting being
There's more to her then what you're seeing.

She creates life in a spiritual dimension
And keeps it alive through physical affection.

Today she's narrowed down to a swipe or a match
A temporary fixture, a one off catch.

Cleopatra and Aphrodite would be saddened to hear
These divine creatures are holding their hearts in fear.

Swipe Left

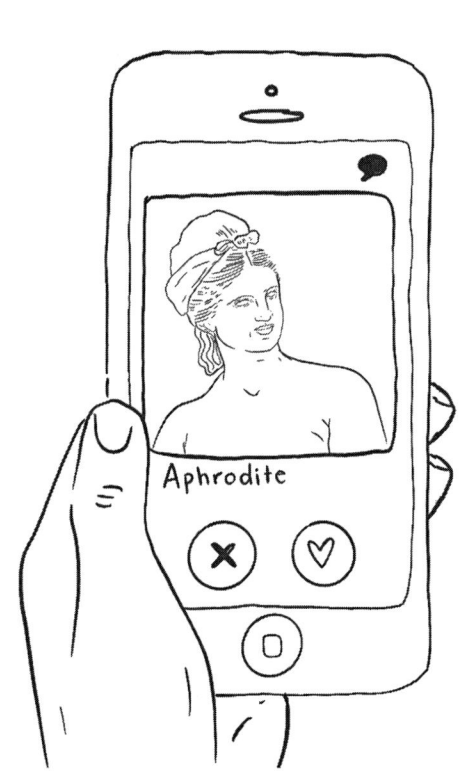

When I hear my love feels sad and alone
I wish I could hold you close and make my heart your home.

To feed your every emotion and your soul
And put your head on my chest and make you feel whole.

When you try be so strong, but you're actually in distress
With me you can be you, I will never think of you any less.

Feeling Whole

To feel emotions is such a beautiful thing
Even if sometimes feel like you have a broken wing.

I wish like King Midas I had the magic touch
And had golden hands so you wouldn't hurt so much.

Touch

Even the stars that glitter so bright
Have scars that are hidden by the night

But their imperfections sparkle
Even in the dark

And continue to shine
Leaving their mark.

Imperfections

A dreamboard with pictures of an unfulfilled dream
Visions that could only be completed if we were a team.

As the whirlwind year comes to an end
And a relationship that went from lovers to friends.

A complicated year full of love, death, life, and distance
And a woman who wanted nothing but persistence.

Never had I shared a homely space with a man before
Because it was a Godly fear, one that I thought would make me feel like a whore.

But it was a beautiful experience waking up next to you
Hearing you breathing next to me was a wonderful view.

But like all good things, this came to an end
What a beautiful chapter, and now difficult to comprehend.

How it ended in such a whirlwind, so quick…
was it a mirage
Or was it something steady and it was our own sabotage?

But like some of your exes you'll speak of me kindly
And chose a new path so quickly and blindly.

But God has mysterious ways of showing us the path
We pick the journey, but only he knows the aftermath.

In this we trust and let the universe do its own thing
And we suddenly realize, we are actually pawns and not kings.

Pawns

Like a nomad
I looked for a heart in my home
And for a home in my heart
And I didn't find either.

Home

I'm sorry that you think I wasn't there for you enough
But being a million miles away from you is so tough.

I didn't leave the house, I cried all day, I washed myself and I said a prayer
But in your mind, you thought I didn't care.

Nothing I could have done would have been enough
Because mourning is such a personal journey, it's so tough.

My heart for you is as pure as ever.

I think of you every second even though you don't think of me
You have a new life now, without me, you see.

New homes

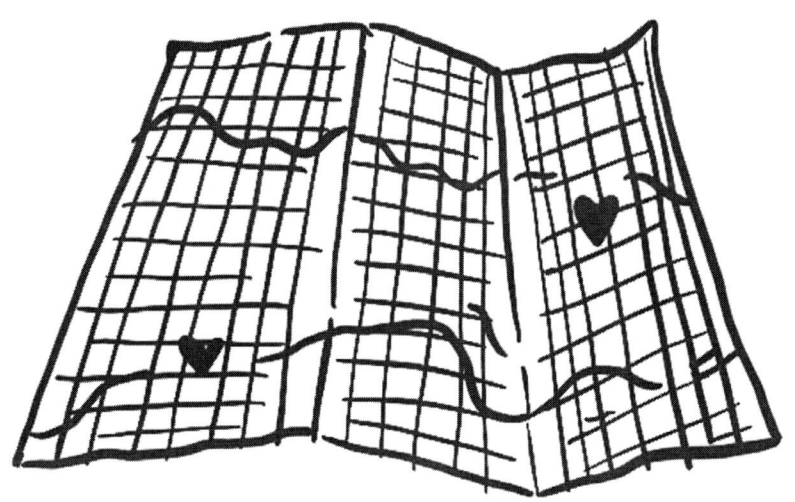

We were on this journey together to teach each
other something
I taught you how to love, you taught me to be a king.

In Buddhism, people come into your life for a reason
It's either forever or for a season.

I pray you heal and find the love that you are looking for
Because I love you and this is me and I can't
offer anything more.

Offerings

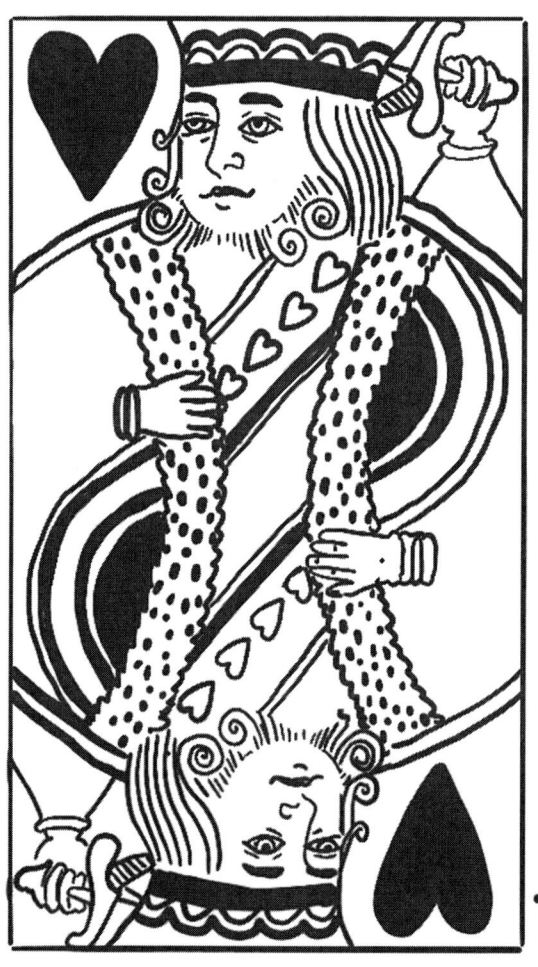

I thought you were my soul mate
I thought you were the one
You were my moon, stars, and sun.

But you were my twin flame
A dangerous pair
A tumultuous toxic affair.

When you were in pain
I would feel it in my bones
Even though we were in different time zones.

The vibration of your voice
Felt so familiar, like home
Whether you were in Luxembourg, Naples, or Rome.

But disappearing on me is not OK
For seven nights and one day.

Slipping Away

I never thought you would mean anything
It was just supposed to be a sterile fling.

Your touch wasn't meant to make me feel
I never knew my heart you would steal.

But we only realize things when they're slipping away
And you still pretend like everything is OK.

Relationships without titles are a trap
A damaging path to the heart, without a map.

So many rules, and yet none at all
Until one of you starts to fall.

No Titles

Spring arrived
When are you coming?

The flowers bloomed
You never came.

You promised you would come
When it snowed
Winter came.

The ice melted
You never came.

The seasons change their mind
And so do you.

But I'm consistent
Like the sky
Always so blue.

Seasons
(Inspired by an Afghan song)

You say I'm so perfect and
I'm love and light
Then what's the reason you want to fight?

You say I'm so perfect
But can't you see
That perfect for you is
All I want to be?

To feel emotions is such a beautiful thing
Even if sometimes you have a broken wing

To heal your scars
I wish I had the Midas touch

And had golden hands
So you wouldn't hurt so much.

All the light you need
Is already inside you

Look within
It's a wonderful view!

Midas Touch

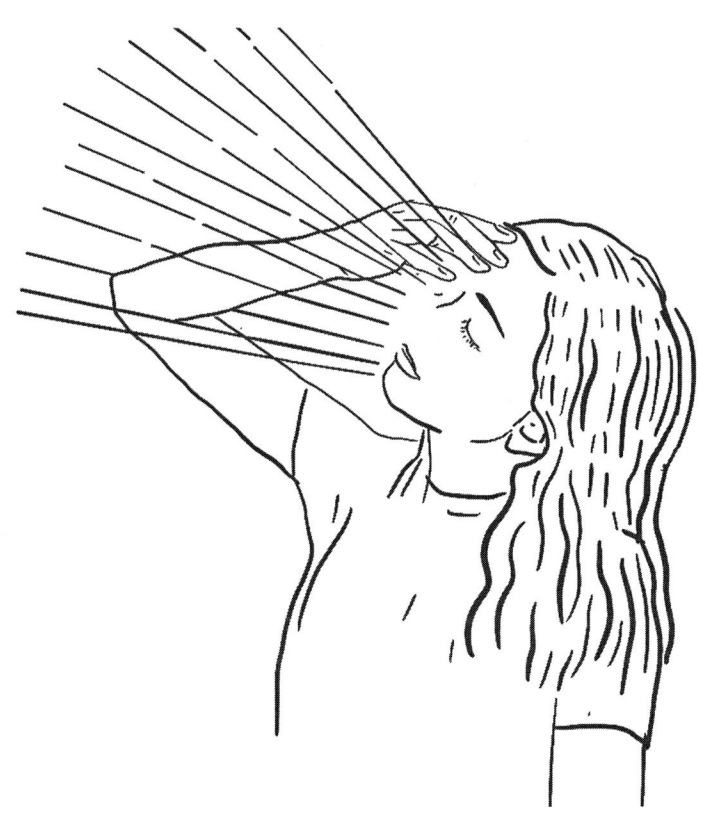

A little garden to plant raw fruits
A steel recycling bin with a chute.

A bench outside to sit and talk
A tree where possums nest, birds squawk.

An Afghan room, red mattresses on the floor
A little library with books galore.

A white crisp couch with a creme throw
A fluffy Persian rug, all the colors of the rainbow.

Paintings and art all over the home
Lapis from Kabul, art from Rome.

Candles from Paris and cushions from Morocco
A rack from Tuscany or Bordeaux.

A pink wall that attracts fengshui and love
A meditation room, for prayers above.

Home

It'll soon be a year since you left
Since my heart was torn away
And I wept and I wept.

I watched as you packed your luggage
Leaving behind me and your baggage.

I made a recording of all your friends
Little did I know that was how it ends.

Boarding a plane with you
But coming back alone
Spending an entire year next to my phone.

Now I'm finally letting go
Books and photos with no tomorrow.

Destiny tearing us apart
8 suitcases and in one was my heart.

Suitcase

Muting and blocking
Unleashing and unlocking

Nasty words and lashing out
Uncertainty and so much doubt

Fiery behavior and a pain in my veins
A love that has me bound in chains

Trying to let go but it's patched in my soul
So much angst, so much turmoil.

Forgotten

Oh heart,

Don't walk the path of danger
Or walk the path of love

But if you do…

Don't tremor
Don't shudder

Be valiant
Fear not

Because the heart is all one's got.

Letter to the Heart

In the time of need you didn't need me
It's not me who you wanted to see.

Where was my place in your current life
For someone you say you wanted as your wife?

I wish you success of the greatest kind
May you rise and rise and have an even greater mind.

May you be blessed with abundance and health
And May you find love to go alongside your wealth.

Blessings

A flower is beautiful when it is given life
love, sunshine, kindness, and water.

Let her bloom in her own wright
Pull her from her roots and she wilts and withers.

Pluck her petals and she pains in silence and slowly fades
Feed her soul with life and love.

Let her grow and rise and rise
For her soil is also yours, you just didn't feel it yet

Petals

Tornados,
Earthquakes,
Storms and Tsunamis,
Even Mother Nature has her crazy days,
I'm just human.

Off Days

Do you love me more than Capri
I would ask you.

Hoping the answer would be
I love you too.

But the moment she managed to get your attention
My name didn't even get a mention.

Who was I to think I could compete with her waves
Her curves, her shores and the women she bathes.

But one thing Capri and I have in common
Your love for us is only seasonal
And then we become foreign.

Capri

This has happened before
And you'll do it again
Whether I'm your girl or your friend.

I love you and I always will

And I'll remember this as a special time
When I was yours and you were mine.

But all good things must come to an end
And maybe this is something we can't mend.

When you finally meet her, you will know
Because you'll do everything in your power
To keep her before she lets go.

Letting Go

Will there ever come a day we meet
Because without you my heart is incomplete.

My bones hurt when I hear your name
I wish we would both stop playing this game.

Do you think of me like I think of you
And think back to the days
When it was just us two?

Just Us Two

You are street smart and wise
Carry trauma in those piercing eyes.

Your beauty irresistible to many
But trauma it is you carry.

A voice of hope for the nation
A fire within
The epitome of determination.

Strength has been woven in your soul
One day your life will be in your control.

Afghan Girl

I am Afghan
What am I worth?
Sometimes it feels like
I was cursed at birth.

Another day
Another life lost
But for how long
And at what cost?

You have become numb
To stories about us
It's just not something
That you want to discuss.

We were let down
From those that were supposed to lead
Watching us
As we continue to bleed

The Worth of an Afghan

I am Afghan
We have more to offer
But sometimes you
Just see me as a bother.
I am Afghan
Where to from here
Safe, healthy, and accepted
Is all I want to be.

I am Afghan
Remember me in your prayers
I promise I am more than
Just my despairs.

Afghan

Will there come a day
When we can return
Without a single worry or concern.

Her lush green mountains slender and curvy
For your undivided attention, she is worthy.

Her beauty is danger, second to none
And her heart, nobody has conquered
Nobody has won.

The history written over her map
But this land of love is a trap.

For it's a love you can never win
A land you can never return to
Just carry her name on your skin.

Expat Afghans

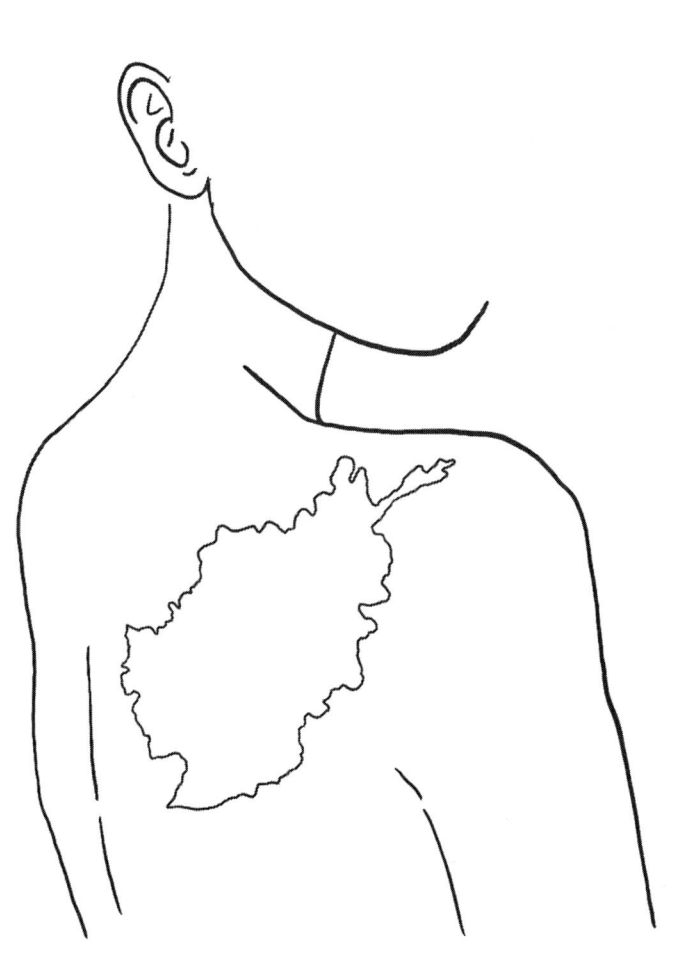

70 million people all displaced
One thing in common: it was one thing we chased.

Safety, a home to keep us warm
A roof to protect us in the storm.

Freedom, a place that gave us our right
A city that let us roam safely in the night.

Identity, a home that gave us back our pride
Somewhere we could call home and not have to hide.

Refugees

Water rising
The word Afghanistan…desensitizing

The mountains crying over the valleys
The death toll, a rising tally

Houses in rubble
Digging through mud
How much water, how much blood

Colorful carpets drowning in thread
Isn't it enough how much they've bled?

Parwan Floods

Somewhere our children could play with a toy and not a tire
Somewhere we can roam free, not trapped behind barbwire.

I'm not a criminal and not a thief
I may look different but we are the same underneath.

If I put my child on a boat, it's out of desperation
Because I was failed, by my very own nation.

I risk my life because I wanted a better one
A nomad, my clothes on my back
And now on the run.
On world refugee day I want you to remember me
And that all a refugee wants, is to be free.

World Refugee Day

I can't wait to smell the Afghan air
Even if it's not fresh
It will smell like home
The scent of the dusty roads will smell familiar
The warmth and the hospitality of the flags at the airport
Standing tall and proud
The anticipation is thrilling
How will she embrace me
The curves in her mountains, how have they changed
The light sunshine in her eyes, how do they continue to glisten
The pain in her roar, how will she voice it.

The sound of helicopters is all I can hear
And the call to prayer, everyone praying without fear
I eat the food without any hesitation
Because this food is in my blood and me being here is out of manifestation.

Returning to Afghanistan

I love how Kabul embraces me
The curves in her mountains and how Mother Nature
lets them be.

Nature is the one thing that continues to glisten
She is the voice of the people and continues to listen.

Embrace of Kabul

Books and pens,
Young minds ready to flourish.

A fertile soil of knowledge,
A society so ready to nourish.

Kabul is a blooming flower,
And a fruitful education is all they desire.

So many obstacles,
So many weeds.

But Afghanistan with continue to sow,
And other talented young minds will grow.

Kabul University

The lion walking with powerful stride
Leading the country with all his pride

His khaki suit and woolen hat
Lines of journalists in awe, waiting to chat

Charisma oozing from his soul
A peaceful Afghanistan, his ultimate goal

Speaking French was his way to charm the west
He was part of our history and for that we are blessed.

The Lion of Panjshir
Ahmad Shah Massoud
9th September 2001

Familiar
When something feels like home,
The nostalgia, when it's one of your own.

Like when the wave returns to the sand,
And you can taste the motherland.

Costume

You are OK
But if you're not OK
Then you should say
What it is that's making you feel this way.

Is it the way you look in your clothes
Or that you feel too far away from your goals
Is it that your boyfriend didn't propose
Or that you have had enough highs, too many lows.

You need to work out why you're feeling this way
Cleanse, focus and then pray
Because whatever you believe in prayer is the solution
It doesn't matter what it's about or part of an institution.

Ground yourself with your feet on the soil
And take your own life in your control
Because you are amazing and you are enough
And this period is already so tough.

You Are OK

For the first time since quarantine…

I went to the beach
This island of heaven was so within reach.

I noticed how different the sand felt on my feet
A free massage from nature, oh what a treat!

I watched as the waves invited me in
But this time he felt different on my skin.

I noticed every movement and touch
I realized how I missed this so much.

Quarantine

Eid is a beautiful shining light
The crescent moon always sparkling bright.

The aroma of oud trails from the mosques
The worshippers sitting together, their legs are crossed.

The little children gather for gifts
from their elders, as they give their hand a kiss.

They grow up running to the breakfast table
Fresh bread, sweet honey, cakes with maple.

With the abundance of laughter, music and dance
Couples are in high spirits, ready to romance.

This is why Eid is such a blessed time of year
Be safe, think of others and spend it without fear.

Eid

Some isolation has let me rediscover myself
To step back and slow down has been good for my health

But I'm most grateful for – one lesson – as I sip from my mug
To never take for granted the pure joy of a hug.

As you scroll through this make believe world
Try and remain silent and undisturbed.

This web is a vortex that can eat you alive
And somehow make you believe your life is so deprived.

The Web

Let it flow on the page
Drink some tea, burn some sage.

Slow down, pick up the pen
Connect to your world within.

Leave the outside universe, it doesn't belong
So much noise, blocking out your inner song.

Pen

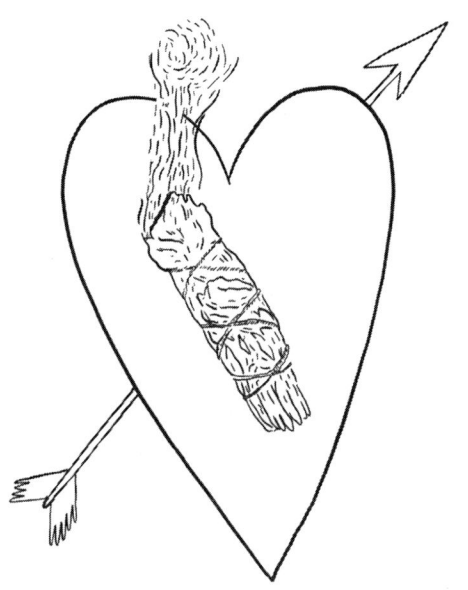

Intoxicated by life and the possibilities of what if
Laughing and dancing to the beat of the drum.

A glimpse of a flashing message on my phone
A flicker of hope in a message.

But then he says, I'm not enough
Is it really me, or should I call his bluff?

Tapping away at my phone to hold onto what we had
Holding onto a hope that is slipping away.

But home is where your heart is
And you can never escape me, I am your home.

Heart & Home

The water was velvet, my skin was silk
A natural reunion, like honey and milk.

The sun was also there to comfort both of us
But it was a party for two, didn't want to cause a fuss.

Oh, how I missed this natural endorphin!
You are his queen, nature your king.

I wish you could see
Some of the inbox messages sent to me.

I just know I'm being watched, every move I make
People are judging every step that I take.

To be the shape that's desired, I'd exercise all day
But I'd also have to change my own DNA.

Maybe I should be earning more money?
Everyone knows wealth makes things more sunny.

If I'd become a famous actor or scientist or big CEO
The feeling of judgement would start to let go.

If I found the man of my dreams and he made me his wife
People would think I've found a perfect girl's life.

If I had a bigger house, a nicer car, and maybe a pool
Would people like me more and think that I'm cool?

Or maybe if I was a loving and nurturing mom
Isn't that what a woman's meant to become?

Of their stern gaze and scrutiny I'd just love to be free!
And I could be if I accept all the judgements coming from me.

Judgements

The mosaic tiles, blue on blue
Bright pink bougainvillea, shining on you.

Tanning oil sliding on the skin
The sun sparkling happiness within.

Souk

Ladies, if you want to feel body confident, do a Turkish bath
It will take your body down a new path.

Your new skin feels like expensive raw silk
And with the scrubs your body moves like organic milk.

When you're lying down and you stare up at the turquoise miniature Persian square
And you breath in deep with all the steam in the air

All that steam and you see one big cloud
And your new body is a gift that makes you proud.

And they scrub and scrub with your string underwear on
When you look down, you celebrate what is gone.

The Hammam is a place for all shapes and sizes
And where your love for the hammam ritual arises.

And when you think of the ottoman women who did this all the time
Their hair smelt like roses and their bodies smelt fine.

For the one hour you're taken back in time
To an empire that enjoyed women and raw wine.

Was it the Romans, the Greeks, or the Turks who started this tradition

Or was it just by man, clean fresh women being their mission?

Hammam

Waking up next to the sound of the sea
Lying on the grainy sand, simple and makeup free.

The mountains and valleys making a perfect backdrop
Had to make a stop for a photo, a headshot.

There's nothing like a weekend amongst Mother Nature
Rejuvenates the soul, gratitude to The Creator.

Nature

Move your hips to the sound of the drum
To feel free, wild, and young
Dance is the only thing that will make you free
To bring you back to you
And me back to me.

Whirl and twirl to the sound of the drum
To feel free, wild and young.

Dance and breathe, the rhythm will set you free
To bring you back to you
An me back to me.

Sufism

That tightness in your chest
That feeling of wearing an anxiety vest.

All this built-up stress…

Take a moment, take a breath
Queen, you're already so blessed.

Tight Chest

You are neither man nor woman
Nor Buddhist nor brahman.

Nor big nor slim
Nor happy nor grim.

You just morph into your soul…
So pure, authentic, and whole.

And your soul doesn't discriminate
Always love, never about hate.

But if only we could mirror ourselves while we sleep
Our everyday lives would be less shallow, and so much more deep.

Sleep

A pandemic that is making it hard to breathe
Lack of air has brought the world to its knees.

The knee that stopped George Floyd from taking a breath
Gasping for air while he was pressed on the neck.

The earth is struggling to breathe as we speak
Toxins, pollution, plastic bottles in creeks.

An elephant just trying to give it's baby air
Cruelly fed crackers, death without care.

We need air to fly our planes above
Experience cultures and visit cities we love.

We all start with our first breath of air
but what's this gift worth if we can't lean to care?

Breath

Anxiety and stress
Cooped up at home
I'm starting to feel so alone.

Straightening hair
Donning a dress
Now looking like a mess.

Walks in fresh air
Enjoying the sun
Today I haven't seen anyone.

Cute gym clothes
Muscles are sore
Checking Instagram, what a bore!

Booking dates
Making plans
Now we have to sit on our hands.

For this virus to win it has to spread.
But I won't help, I'm at home instead.

Covid

For the people I could infect
For my friends and family
For myself
And for all the things I miss…
staying at home.

Covid

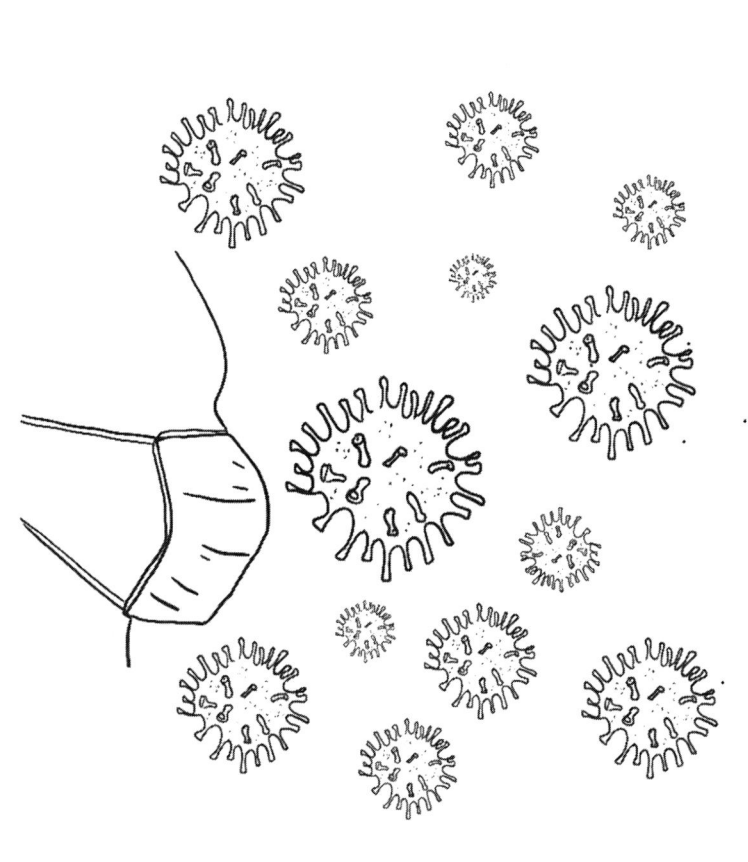

Dear younger Maz,

Life teaches great wisdom as you make your way
Let me share some with you now, on this your 10th birthday.

Primary school is such a joy, so be sure to have fun
Play in a hat, protect your skin from damage from the sun.

Try not to worry about what the all bullies say at school
It's the hurt kids who tend to be so cruel.

In high-school, commit, work hard, embrace this chance to grow
Be free, explore, don't hold mistakes, learn from them…let go.

You shouldn't stress about little things like those freckles on your face
Given time such qualities you'll happily embrace.

Don't be disheartened that your path isn't clear yet
Just avoid credit cards and unnecessarily debt.

Be respectful of your parents' rules, that will pay off later
Be grateful for your opportunities, give thanks to your creator.

Embrace your spirituality and get to know your higher purpose
The universe is on your side, have faith, don't be nervous.

Eat fresh food and exercise, your body's all you really own
Share often and be generous…a gift, not a loan.

Don't be judgmental and always respect other people
Negative thoughts blacken your heart, it's an unwanted evil.

Be proud of your curves and the way they suit your shape
Love your parents without question,
not all heroes wear a cape.

Younger Maz

You'll grow in confidence with your looks more and more as you age
But remember the beauty's right there at every single stage.

Have faith as you chase your goals, believe you'll find a way
A home and love and happiness…just take it day by day.

So, little Maz, take these thoughts and apply them to your life
They'll help to keep the ghosts at bay and keep you out of strife.

Years from now I know each word will make perfect sense, you'll see
Because today as you celebrate your birthday again, little Maz, you're me.

To Little Maz

But who knows what the universe has in store
But all I know is, of your love I want more.

Flying economy I'm all on board
But it wouldn't be my first choice if I could afford.

The man next to me keeps blowing his nose
And the one in front is cleaning his toes.

My throat is starting to hurt or is it in my head
Why can't I just get a seat with a bed?

The goal is to always fly business or first
Where they give you champagne to quench your thirst.

I don't eat on the plane, no, thank you
It causes blockages, you know this too.

The man next to me, there he goes ag-ain
Why can't you just blow your nose in the toilet, you pain?

There's a crying child also on board
Will I get any sleep, oh lord?

OK, there seat 54J goes blowing his nose
Why on earth is his nose watering like a hose?

Oh, there he goes again, now he's moved onto cough-ing
Sounds like a symphony, he may as well sing.

I can't wait to finally land
And be in my bed in the land of the sand.

Be a little considerate, seat 54J
We've only just taken off, but I'm over this flight already, OK?

Sitting amongst the rustling of the trees,
Loving restaurants like these.

With thousands of branches all intertwined
And lanterns too, so glad it was here that we dined.

There's a man walking around spreading coal and bukhoor,
There's now a mist in the air, this place is authentic to the core.

Plates made from bamboo and wood,
Yes, we'll be back, the food was so good.

Beirut, your beautiful bustling city is hurting today
The world is on their knees, for you they pray.

A city so full of music and light
And today your people, so tired of the fight.

A people so full of life and love
The coffee shops full, people feeding the pigeons and doves.

The coastline such a sight to see
Nowhere else the Lebanese people would want to be.

The Paris of the Middle East, you are bleeding
You've broken our hearts, the world is grieving.

Beirut

Knee on neck,
I can't breathe
All you see is my color
And not what is underneath.

Knee on neck
I can't breathe
Please let go
I have children to feed.

Knee on neck
I can't breathe
I don't want my family
To have to grieve.

Knee of neck
I can't breathe
Stop pressing on me
For 8 mins and 46 seconds, please.

Knee on neck
I can't breathe
Mama, help me
Tell them to stop, please!
Knee on neck
I can't breathe
It might be too late
To hear apologies.

Knee on neck
I can't breathe
Say my name
So my life wasn't misconceived.

George Floyd

She is graceful and elegant and moves with stride
She holds herself with dignity and pride.

She is educated, smart, and has a voice
And is a middle eastern woman who is given choice.

She is soft and strong, delicate but in control
She has substance and charisma and has her own goal.

When she walks past, she leaves a beautiful trail
Her oud, the vanilla and wood, and her beautiful veil.

Emirati Women's day is all about celebration
Of the men and women that helped built this beautiful nation.

Emirati Woman

Watching the bubbles rise in a bath
Or counting the lines while walking on the path

The first bite of a chocolate mud cake
Or when nobody notices when you make a mistake

Choosing flowers for the house from the local store
Or staring at the earrings through a window at Dior

The smell of a package when it first arrives
Baking a cake and watching it rise

The way my body aches after doing some squats
Or day dreaming about buying a yacht

The way my skin feels when I wash off a mask
The way my swimmers look when in the sun I bask

I love what these little things bring
Happiness, love, and satisfaction within.

Little Things

I was born in a garden.

In my first breaths, I was connected to earth,
Understanding basic necessities, their worth.

Not a single hospital bed in sight,
Just a refugee mother, tired of the fight.

No doctors or nurses or bouquets around,
My queen mother deserves to be crowned.

I was born in a garden.
My mother was the only rose in sight.

My Birth

When we met our love was a seed.
Ready to burst into life,
To bloom and to feed.

How did we become a choking weed overgrown?

Wishing our love had never been sown.

Seeds

Brought you home when you were the size of my palm,
You instantly made us smitten with your sense of charm.

Guard the house like it was your fort,
Follow us around like it was a sport.

Chew on socks for hours on end,
Brought so much joy, my best friend.

Your glistening eyes, full of life,
To introduce you, when I became someone's wife.

Your furry touch gave abundant love,
Fly high now, my little white dove.

Zorro

Trying to catch a rainbow,
Or chasing a reflective shadow,

Counting particles of sand,
Or if it's me you're trying to understand,

I'm just as confused,
Leaving hearts a little bruised.

Rainbows

You are so pretty… but
You should change your hair color
It's not right
Dye it softer, not dark like the night.

Oh and

I don't like your makeup
You should wear less
More subtle, less excess.

And while you're at it…

Your eyeliner is not appealing
If it wore a brown it would be more appeasing.

And also
Is there something wrong with your face

Between your eyes and forehead
There's a huge space.

And there's your lips…

Which are nice
But you should wear more pink
Well, that's what I think.

And also…

Your body is curvy
But you should run
If you want it more perky.

Pretty